Champagne
the
spirit
of
celebration

by Sara Slavin and Karl Petzke

Art Direction, Styling : Sara Slavin
Photography : Karl Petzke
Text : Peggy Knickerbocker
Design : Morla Design
Recipes, Food Styling : Sandra Cook

CHRONICLE BOOKS
SAN FRANCISCO

Page 4 constitutes a continuation of the copyright page.

Printed in Hong Kong.

Book and cover design:
Morla Design, Inc., San Francisco

Library of Congress Cataloging-in-Publication Data:
Slavin, Sara. Champagne : the spirit of celebration/
by Sara Slavin and Karl Petzke.
p. cm.
Includes bibliographical references and index.
ISBN 0-8118-0928-5 (pbk)
ISBN 0-8118-0903-X (HC)
1. Champagne (Wine) I. Petzke, Karl. II. Title.
TP555.S63 1995
641.2'224–dc20   94-41852
                  CIP

Distributed in Canada by Raincoast Books,
8680 Cambie Street,
Vancouver, B.C. V6P 6M9

10 9 8 7 6 5 4 3 2 1

Chronicle Books
275 Fifth Street
San Francisco, CA 94103

7

Earth

36

Nectar

63

Stars

Bibliography

1. *Champagne*, Andre L. Simon, McGraw-Hill, New York, 1962
2. *The Story of Champagne*, Nicholas Faith, Facts on File, New York, 1989
3. *Drinking Champagne and Brandy*, Youngman Carter, Hastings House, Great Britain, 1967
4. *In Praise of Wine and Certain Noble Spirits*, Alec Waugh, William Sloane Associates, New York, 1959

Credits

A book happens as a result of vision, chemistry, and collaboration–therefore we raise our glasses and toast the following who are responsible for the support and production of *Champagne*. ♦ To Nion McEvoy, Charlotte Stone, and Michael Carabetta of Chronicle Books, for their ongoing encouragement, insight, and support. ♦ To Jennifer Morla, designer of our dreams, for taking this project way past our very high expectations and always expanding the art of design. ♦ To Sandra Cook for rising to, and far above, the occasion with the creativity of your recipes, artistry of your styling, and the sweetness of your soul. ♦ To Peggy Knickerbocker for turning your love and knowledge of Champagne into vintage words and filling them with your humor, dedication, and spirit. ♦ To the warm and generous people at the great Champagne houses of France. At Moët et Chandon: Ghislane Simon, at G. H. Mumm et Cie: Agnes Laplanché and Rachell Daumagnan, and at Veuve Clicquot: Roselyn de Casteja and Valerie Chaumont. Thank you all for your graciousness, hospitality, knowledge, and for always keeping our glasses full. ♦ To Chuck Hayward of the Jug Shop in San Francisco for blazing our trail into the Champagne region of France. ♦ To the staff of Morla Design, especially Craig Bailey, for their patience and enthusiasm. ♦ And to our friends, colleagues, and families who are always there for us: Steven Barclay, Nilus de Matran, Melanie Fife, Kathryn Kleinman, Deborah Jones, Saul Gropman, Wendi Nordeck, Carlos Stelmach, Bertie Walter, Emily Luchetti and Star's Cafe, Sonoma Grapevines, Richard Jeoffrey of Dom Pérignon, Dawnine Dyer at Domaine Chandon, Isabelle Rosenzweig at Veuve Clicquot in New York, and to the shops Fillamento, Sue Fisher-King, and Paul Bauer of San Francisco for the use of their beautiful things and their kindness. – *Sara Slavin and Karl Petzke*

Especially to Lillian Moss, Kate Slavin, Sybil Slavin, and Mark Steisel for always being there. – S.S.

To my parents Georgiann Petzke and Alfred Petzke for a lifetime of love and support. – K.P.

This book is dedicated to Dom Pérignon and Madame Clicquot.

Earth

*I*t only takes one sip of champagne for the spirit to feel miraculously restored, elegant, frivolous, chic, and extravagant. Champagne can soothe the soul, enliven the heart, and propel even the most reserved person into lively conversation or onto the dance floor. Romance may be ignited; certainly the chances of a kiss are more likely.

Champagne has launched millions of ships and a billion celebrations. Champagne stimulates the appetite, dispels timidity, overcomes sorrow. It is a friend for life—at weddings, christenings, everywhere and anytime life bursts into song.

The magic of champagne begins before the first sip; it begins with the first sigh of the cork. If a party is seen as a concert, and the guests as the musicians, champagne is the conductor, orchestrating its harmony, tone, and rhythm.

Champagne was the wine the rich and privileged drank during Napoleon III's reign; it was the wine that sparkled in the glasses of the tsars and dukes of imperial Russia. Champagne was glamorized by movie stars and is even rumored to have been used by Marilyn Monroe for her baths. Making timid men and women aspire well beyond their normal constraints, champagne has, taken in proper quantities, the distinct quality of urging the heart to soar.

Chalk in the soil in the Champagne region of France gives champagne its unique nature, its acidity, and its character. Vineyards are planted only in areas that have this snowy-white limestone. The excellent drainage of this porous chalk, its rich and nutritious top layers of soil, and the auspicious microclimate of the region make growing grapes for champagne ideal.

In this region near Paris, wherever there is limestone topped with soil composed of mineral deposits and fossils of ancient marine life, there are vineyards. The value of the snowy-white chalk is so high that vines are planted to the rim of most villages in Champagne. Not a chalky hectare is wasted —vines are sometimes planted right up to the back door of a shop or restaurant.

"Chalk fragments in the soil reflect light back into the foliage of the vine," and, according to one of the most noted champagne writers, Patrick Forbes, "from an aesthetic point of view, the phenomenon is astounding; it tones down colors, softens outlines, and gives the countryside a hazy, out of focus look, reminiscent of an Impressionist painting."

Years ago, in the Champagne region, Roman slaves excavated limestone quarries for building material. Today those hundreds of miles of excavated chalk are used as the caves that house hundreds of millions of bottles of champagne.

$\mathcal{C}$hampagne is usually more expensive than other wines simply because it is harder to make. The *méthode champenoise* is the traditional French champagne method for producing sparkling wines. It is an intricate and labor intensive procedure that involves a series of stringent regulations that bring the grape from the vine to the bottle—pressing, fermentation, blending, yeast aging, bottling, riddling, disgorging, dosage, and, finally, corking.

The grapes, mainly pinot noir, with varying percentages of pinot meunier and chardonnay, are picked in late summer or early fall and then are quickly pressed to yield a juice with minimal color. The resulting juice, or "must," is stored in great vats where the first fermentation occurs. During this primary fermentation, the yeast feeds on the natural sugar present in the must and converts it to alcohol and carbon dioxide gas.

Following this fermentation the wine is filtered to remove sediment and blended with reserve wine from previous years. For most champagnes, the *chef de cave* of each house determines what percentage of older wines is to be blended into the *cuvée* (assembling of the best reserve wine) that will produce a final product that is consistent with the style of the specific house. An exception to this process occurs in certain years when the grapes produce an extraordinary wine that the *chef de cave* decides to call "vintage." In France that means 100 percent of the grapes from one year go into a vintage release—no blending from previous years. But in California, a vintage year means 95 percent of the vintage year grapes are blended with the addition of 5 percent from a previous year's blend.

The second fermentation occurs in the bottle. In order to bring it about, sugar and yeast are added to the wine. The bottle is temporarily capped and stored to mature for a few months to six years or more. When the wine has aged satisfactorily, the bottles are placed in racks, necks pointing downward, to be twisted by hand or machines. This is done so the sediment (the dead yeast cells that have been deposited on the sides of the bottles) will dislodge and settle upon the crown cap.

In the early 19th century La Veuve Cliquot "the Widow," who was widowed at age twenty-seven, took over and vastly expanded and improved the house of her husband, François. She invented this process, called "riddling" or *remauge*, that totally changed the look and

taste of champagne. Before her refinement, champagne was a cloudy drink, full of sediment, which is why frosted glasses were fashionable, hiding the imperfections in the wine.

In spite of the fact that she had no scientific background, Madame Cliquot had discovered a way to get rid of the sediment right at her kitchen table. She angled holes into the table so the bottles could stand on their heads after aging, nudging the sediment to slide down the neck to the cork. Since some sediment still clung to the sides of the bottle, she gave the bottle a slight twist, just enough to ease the sediment on its way to the cork where it could then be consolidated and removed. Riddlers have used this technique ever since, and some houses now use computerized gyropalettes that twist the bottles more quickly than the more time-consuming, traditional method.

The final step in the long and involved process of champagne making is *dégorgement* (disgorgement). Here the neck of the bottle is chilled in a brine solution so the sediment coagulates as a frozen plug resting behind the cap. It is popped out when the cap is removed quickly and skillfully. Before the final cork is inserted, a small amount of sugar dissolved in still wine (*liqueur d'expédition*) is added, the amount of which determines whether the champagne will be brut, extra sec, or sec. This whole procedure takes place in a matter of seconds. After this stage, the bottle is labeled and shelved until it goes to market. Fermentation ceases at this stage of *dégorgement*, and no further activity occurs in the bottle. This is why champagne does not improve, as most good things do, with age.

In the Champagne country of France, rosebushes are as much a signature of the landscape as grapevines. They are seen everywhere—on the road between villages, at the end of a row of grapes, and lushly arranged in every house and restaurant.

Rosebushes have something in common with grapevines: both are susceptible to a powdery mildew (genus *Oidium*). That is why, over the years, rosebushes have been planted at the ends of rows of grapes. Like a canary in a coal mine, rosebushes usually get hit by the mildew first, warning grape growers to hastily treat their vines. Of course, today's growers have more reliable methods for diagnosing problems, but the tradition of planting roses endures.

The rose is a symbol from medieval times of the Blessed Mother, a good omen for crops. When the rosebush is planted at the end of a row of grapevines, it adds spiritual value to what will become a commercial commodity. Rosebushes are colorful parentheses to the rows of gnarly vines, softening the landscape with a graceful sense of fertility and expansion.

Grilled Nectarines with Prosciutto

Smoky, sweet, slightly salty, crisp, and soft—all of these qualities blend together to make a memorable appetizer or a luscious addition to a salad. While the coals heat, chill the champagne.

4 firm (but not hard) nectarines
12 thin slices prosciutto
8 6-inch-long bamboo skewers
   soaked in water for 20 minutes
2 tablespoons melted butter
4 lime wedges
2 tablespoons chopped fresh mint

Wash, dry, and slice each nectarine into 6 wedges. Tear the prosciutto slices in half lengthwise and wrap a thin strip around each nectarine wedge. Place 3 wedges of nectarine on each skewer. Brush each skewer with some of the butter and grill over low coals for 10 minutes, turning once. Sprinkle each skewer with some lime juice and some mint. Serves 4 as an appetizer or a side dish.

"Champagne app[lies]
a murmur of foa[m]
of air providing [...]
to birthday and [...]
banquets, compl[...]
truffles from [...]

...ared in its turn,

..., leaping pearls

... accompaniment

...irst Communion

...enting the gray

...a Puisaye ..."

Colette, translated by Derek Coltman

In order to demystify the words on the labels that indicate the level of sweetness or dryness of a particular champagne, it is helpful to understand the process of dosage. The *liqueur d'expédition*, or "dosage," is a solution of sugar dissolved in wine. It is added after the disgorgement and determines the sweetness or dryness level of the sparkling wine. Without a dosage, the wine would be too austere for most tastes. The degree of sweetness varies with the style desired by the *chef de cave* and the tradition of the house.

Brut is the driest of sparkling wines. While some people think the best time to drink it is before dinner, one of the charms of sparkling wine is you can drink it anytime of day.

Extra dry or extra sec is somewhat sweeter than brut and goes well with desserts or wedding cakes.

Sec means "dry" in French, but in the case of sparkling wines, it means "moderately dry" or "slightly sweet."

Demi sec is rarely seen in the United States. It is the sweetest sparkling wine.

Blanc de Blanc is made of only white chardonnay grapes. It refers to white wine of white grapes.

Blanc de noir is white wine made with black, or *noir*, grapes or pinot noir grapes. It is usually fruitier than blanc de blanc and often has a deeper hue as well.

The making of sparkling wines in California almost coincided with the discovery of gold, just in time for the miners to celebrate their glittering strike.

The first California sparkling wine was probably made in San Gabriel, in Southern California, around 1850. It was only slightly later that the Franciscan padres near San Francisco began making wine with mission grapes. Just one hundred years earlier, their brothers in France, led by Dom Pérignon, the Benedictine monk and "the father of champagne," were pursuing the cultivation and improvement of the bubbly wine.

In 1862 California pioneer and statesman General Vallejo produced a sparkling wine that won a prize at the Sonoma State Fair. The fruity mission grapes were really too sweet and created, in the second fermentation, too much carbon dioxide, causing a large percentage of bottles to burst. Soon after, French wine makers brought their techniques to California. Then, with the Franco-Prussian War (1870–1871) in full swing in Europe, shipments of champagne to the

United States were stalled, and Americans were left with only one option—domestic sparkling wines from California.

In the meantime, General Vallejo's son-in-law, Arpad Haraszthy, used a successful combination of grapes, including riesling, muscatel, and zinfandel, instead of the explosive mission grapes. In 1867 he ended up with a much sought after champagne called Eclipse. Korbel, Italian Swiss Colony, and Paul Masson followed shortly thereafter by producing some very respectable sparkling wines.

It wasn't until one hundred years later that the first notable production of champagne since Prohibition got underway. Up until that point the *charmat* method (where fermentation occurs in the tank rather than the bottle) had been widely used. Hanns Kornell in the early 1950s, Schramsberg in the 1960s, and later, Mirassou began producing *méthode champenoise* sparkling wines of style, balance, and good taste. Then in 1973 a few of the major French champagne houses opened outposts around the Napa Valley. Moët-Hennessey came first with Domaine Chandon, followed by Piper-Heidsieck in nearby Healdsburg, Mumm, and Taittinger (under the name of Domaine Carneros).

While some California houses still employ the *charmat* style, the big houses with associations in France use the traditional *méthode champenoise* (fermenting the wine in the bottle). There are a handful of exquisite small houses in California that also use the French method. These houses include Robert Hunter, Van der Kamp, Scharfenberger, Iron Horse, Shadow Creek Cellars, and two Spanish houses—Gloria Ferrer and Cordorniu. They make wines with an identity and dignity of their own that are in no way second-best to French champagne.

The identity of a wine is determined by a combination of agriculture, geography, atmospheric conditions, and the skill of the wine maker. It is not the intention of California houses to copy French champagnes. It would be impossible anyway, because the land and climate of California differ so wildly from the chalky soil and chilly air of the banks of the Marne in Champagne. California is now producing, after just two decades, exceptional sparkling wines, such as Domaine Chandon's outstanding NV Reserve, that year after year become more secure and dignified.

The autumn light in Milan at cocktail hour has a hazy persimmon glow—a mingling of the diminishing light and the unfortunate detritus of industrial residue. We'd spent all day tracking down the best truffles in town and decided to celebrate—to prolong the gratification that we knew our first bite of truffle would bring. We stopped, not far from Monte Napoleone, at a little bar with wicker seats under an awning. When we saw our neighbors toasting each other with a drink the color of the burned pink sky, we asked the waiter for one just like it. In tall, graceful glasses, we were served a combination of pulverized peaches and sparkling Italian wine. It was sublime, the perfect ending to summer, the perfect beginning to autumn. It was heady, it was romantic, it was sweet and musty all at once. It was a Bellini!

The air at harvest time is heavy, sweet, musty, and fruity. Early in the mornings, in the early fall in the Champagne region of France, teams of grape pickers enter the vineyards. They drive along roads, cut like white ribbons through the ripened vines. Every day the cellar master declares an area ready for harvesting, and the teams begin their work. The pickers work quickly, each with his or her own predetermined task. The work is backbreaking, and the vines have been manicured to facilitate easier picking. As the lingering warmth of late summer mingles with the impending chill of fall, the lovely, luscious vines are methodically picked clean. The mornings are cold, often foggy or even rainy, and the workers anxiously await the break in their day when the lunches of fresh sausages, lentils, assorted salads, grainy breads, cheeses, and, of course, local wines are brought to them. The vines rustle quietly as the constant banter of the pickers fills the air.

The ripened fruit is always picked by hand— every grape—resisting the modern alternatives available. First the clusters are cut and tossed into small plastic buckets. They are in turn emptied into large plastic cartons, which are loaded immediately onto trucks that transport this bounty to the waiting presshouse. The arrival of the grapes at the presshouse is a highly anticipated event. Here too, teams of workers await the crop. In most of the presshouses, Champagne growers

still rely on traditional hydraulic presses, caging the soon-to-be pressed grapes in wooden frames. As the grapes arrive, the presshouse workers unload the cartons and systematically begin loading each press, pressing only one kind of grape at a time. Each press, by law, will hold exactly 4000 kilos (8800 pounds) of harvested grapes and will produce 2050 kilos (4500 pounds) of first-press (*cuvée*) juice and 500 kilos (1100 pounds) of the second (*taille*). After each single pressing, the press is thoroughly cleared of the skins, leaves, and stems, and it is washed to begin the process again. This process continues until the amount of grapes allowed by law for each hectare has been met. At that point the harvest is over.

Now it's time for gravity and science to take over. Most presses sit above a sublevel of tanks. As the sweet, musty juice runs from the presses, it is directed, by design, to spill to the tanks below to begin the transformation from juice to wine. As the newly crushed liquid sits in these tanks, it begins its fermentation process and separates itself from the remaining sediment and unwanted particles. When the juice has completed this separation, it is ready to be pumped into trucks that will transport it to the Champagne houses, both grand and small, to become the most potable, controlled bubbling substance on earth.

Nectar

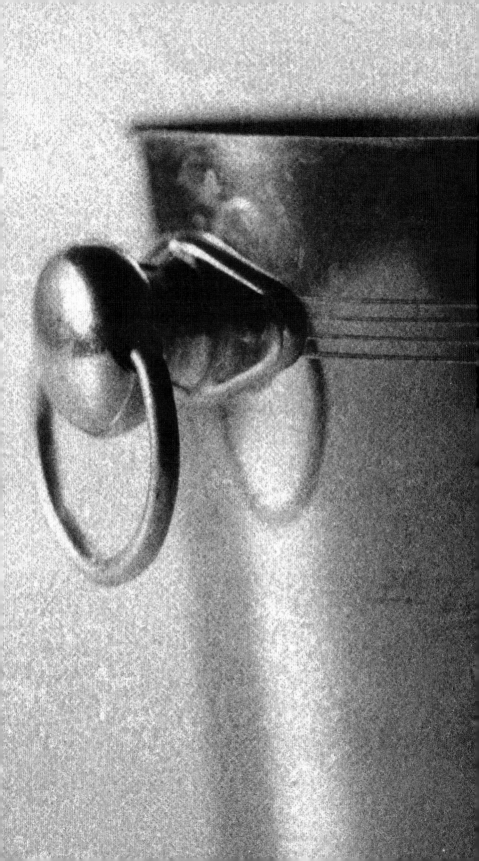

$\mathcal{I}$n the Champagne region of France, most wine makers use three types of grapes for making champagne: pinot noir, to impart body and aging ability; pinot meunier, for fruitiness; and the soigné chardonnay, for a soupçon of elegance and finesse. Just as the distinctive qualities of a cassoulet are based on the chef's unique approach to the ingredients, the distinguishing characteristics of champagne are based on the champagne maker's unique approach to the grapes. Each house furtively guards its recipe for *assemblage* (the mixing together of this year's grapes with those reserve wines of previous vintages) that results in a non-vintage champagne, or a *non millésime*.

Luxury labels are only those champagnes bottled during an exceptional *millésime*, or "vintage year," such as Moët et Chandon's Dom Pérignon, Veuve Clicquot's La Grande Dame, or Roederer's Cristal. The composition of a champagne distinguished by a luxury label, indicating a vintage year, normally uses 60 percent pinot noir and 40 percent chardonnay. The pinot meunier is shipped in these expensive bottles. Blanc de blancs are

produced only from chardonnay and can be found in Krug's Clos du Mesnil and Taittinger's Comtes de Champagne.

While non-vintage champagne is a blend of sometimes as many as seventy to eighty wines from different years and vineyards, vintage champagne is a blend of wines from one extremely good year. It is up to the wine maker at each house to determine whether the wine of a certain year justifies a vintage. The date on the vintage bottle is the year the grapes were picked. While it isn't always noted, another important date for champagne is the date it was disgorged—the date fermentation stopped. *Méthode champenoise* wines are ready to drink when they are shipped to market.

"There was a flood of rosy - mauve champagne flowing from room to purple room, and in this flood floated dozens of beautiful pink gigolos in which le Tout Paris abounds. We stood dizzily at the window watching a pretty purple sunset dis appear behind the grey stone of the Ritz Hotel."

Ned Rorem, *The Paris Diary of Ned Rorem*

Champagne Melon with Smoked Trout

This is a wonderful dish, especially when summer melons are at their peak, making it a delightful blend of sweet and smoky tastes.

1/4 honeydew melon
1/4 cantaloupe
2 cups champagne
2 boneless smoked trouts
1 tablespoon fresh lemon juice
4 tablespoons chopped red and
    green onion

Remove the *rinds* of the melons. Slice each melon section very thin and place in a shallow casserole dish. Pour the champagne over the melon slices and allow to stand for 1 hour. Chill.

Remove any skin from the trouts and crumble the trout meat into a small bowl. Mix the *lemon juice* and onion with the trout. Remove melon slices from champagne and arrange equal parts of honeydew and cantaloupe on 4 chilled plates. *Sprinkle* the trout mixture over the chilled melon slices and serve. Serves 4.

Leftover champagne, if you can imagine such a thing, is good to cook with. Poach fish, prawns, or mussels with it. Simmer chicken breasts in it with herbs and shallots. Cook apples in it for an applesauce that sparkles. Add leftover champagne to your eggs before scrambling them into a delicious omelet with lobster meat and chopped green onion. Cook fennel sausage and cabbage in champagne and add a little crumbled bacon and blue cheese for a warm, wintery salad. Make a palate-cleansing sorbet or enliven a late summer fruit salad with the leftover bubbly wine.

In the absence of a champagne corker, you can still reserve the bubbles by dangling the handle of a silver spoon into the neck of a bottle; for some magical reason, the wine will remain lively for a few hours.

To christen ships in pagan times, humans were sacrificed by the Vikings as gifts to the gods. Later, to ensure good will, it was enough to pour wine on the ground as a ship was about to embark. In the eighteenth century, the French started to use the elegant and celebratory champagne to launch ships.

One might assume the champagne bottle would break easily, since its contents are under such pressure. But the truth is the champagne bottle is almost indestructible, designed so explosions will be avoided during fermentation. That is why you often see people whacking away at ship bows, frustrated because the bottle simply will not break.

The world's largest champagne bottle, according to the *Guinness Book of Records*, was recently used by Lauren Bacall to christen the huge passenger ship *Monarch of the Seas*. (The bottle was called a "sovereign" because the ship it was first used to christen was called *Sovereign of the Seas*.) The bottle stands three feet high, weighs seventy-seven pounds, and holds about three cases of regular-size bottles. No chances were taken here: an elaborate system of pulleys and ropes was used to hoist up the bottle encased in a net so that Bacall could simply snip the cord. When she did, the bottle released, smashed against the ship, and broke.

Champagne Poached Salmon

A delicate, healthful way to prepare salmon. You may want to elaborate with your own sauce, or keep it simple with just a squeeze of lemon.

2 teaspoons olive oil
2 7-ounce salmon steaks
1/2 cup water
2 cups champagne
1/2 cup green onions, chopped
1/4 cup chopped celery
1 teaspoon cracked black
   peppercorns

Coat the surface of a medium-sized skillet with the olive oil and place the *salmon steaks* in the skillet. In a small saucepan combine the remaining ingredients and bring to just before boiling point. Pour the sauce over the fish in the skillet and *simmer* covered over low to medium heat for **8 minutes**. Remove fish from skillet with slotted spatula and serve either warm or chilled with a *wedge of lemon*. Serves 2.

How to Open a Bottle of Champagne

1. Remove only enough of the foil to get to the twisted wire hood.

2. Hold the bottle at a forty-five degree angle with its mouth nearest the first champagne glass to be filled.

3. Hold the cork and gently turn the bottle in one direction. Turn the bottle not the cork.

4. The cork should not pop. "The ear's gain is the palate's loss." Enormous effort has gone into putting the bubbles in the champagne. Why waste bubbles on the cork?

5. The sound of a perfectly opened bottle should be as gentle as a sigh.

Storing Champagne

The icebox is not the ideal spot to store champagne because after a few months the cork starts to loose its elasticity and shrink. This could cause the wine to become a bit bitter. It's never a good idea to store champagne on the door of the refrigerator because of the constant opening and closing. It is better off in a cellar or on a shelf on its side, but only for a short period of time, as time does not enhance the taste of champagne. Better yet, drink your bubbly as soon as you've chilled it. Plunging a bottle of champagne into a bucket of ice and water for twenty to thirty minutes will do the same thing as two to three hours in the refrigerator. Both methods will bring the temperature to forty-five degrees and that is perfect for serving.

Champagne Grilled Leeks

An elegant alternative to a salad. Simple, subtle, and tangy with crumbled feta cheese, leeks have a classic flavor.

6 medium-sized leeks
2 tablespoons olive oil
1 cup fresh thyme,
   roughly chopped
2 cups champagne
1 cup chicken stock
1 cup crumbled feta cheese
salt and pepper to taste

Trim the tops and bottoms of the leeks, leaving approximately 2 to 3 inches of green above the white part of the leek. From the center of the trimmed leek, make several lengthwise slices toward the *green of the leek*. Rinse leeks thoroughly.

In a large sauté pan, heat the olive oil over medium heat. When oil is hot add the **thyme** and stir for 1 minute. Add the leeks and sauté for 3 minutes, until lightly golden on several sides. Add the champagne and the stock and simmer leeks until tender, 8 minutes. Remove leeks from pan and set aside.

Continue to **simmer** sauce remaining in pan until reduced by one half. Meanwhile, grill leeks over medium-hot charcoal fire for 8 to 10 minutes, turning several times. Remove leeks from *grill* and slice in half lengthwise. Serve immediately, adding some feta and bit of the reduced sauce to each serving. Season with salt and pepper. Serves 2 to 4.

It is universally accepted that Dom Pérignon is the "father of champagne." In the late seventeenth century, as cellar master of the Benedictine Abbey of Hautvillers, on the land where Moët et Chandon now sits, Dom Pérignon initiated the method for making champagne as it is still done today. He transformed the still, opaque white or red wines of Champagne into the famous sparkling wine of the Court of Louis XIV.

Every year, in the Champagne region, wine had the unusual tendency to re-ferment in the spring following the vintage. For a while, this tendency was not appreciated. But Dom Pérignon found a way to keep the bubbles in and capitalized upon it. Instead of using pieces of wood wrapped in hemp and dipped in olive oil, he found that corks would tightly seal a bottle of wine that had a tendency to sparkle. He secured the corks with string to keep the bubbles in the bottles. If the glass bottles did not explode under the pressure, then carbon dioxide would dissolve in the wine and make it sparkling.

One of the most famous exclamations of champagne folklore is said to have been uttered by the blind Dom Pérignon when he opened his first successful bottle, "Brothers, come quickly, I am drinking stars!"

Champagne Risotto with Wild Mushrooms

Mushrooms give this dish an earthy flavor and the champagne brings a subtle elegance to taste. Risotto is a most basic dish enhanced by fine ingredients.

4 cups beef broth

3 1/2 tablespoons unsalted butter

1/2 pound wild mushrooms (morel, shiitake, etc.), stemmed and sliced

2 tablespoons finely minced shallots

1 1/2 cups arborio rice

1 1/4 cups champagne

1/4 cup half and half

1/4 cup grated parmesan cheese

1 tablespoon fresh parsley, chopped

Heat **broth** to a simmer and let simmer until later. Meanwhile, in a medium-sized sauté pan, melt 2 tablespoons of the butter. When butter begins to foam, add the mushrooms and sauté for 3 to 5 minutes. Remove from the heat and set aside.

Place the remaining butter in a large heavy-bottomed sauce pan and sauté the **shallots** until soft, about 1 to 2 minutes. Add the rice and stir for 1 minute to coat with the butter-shallot mixture. Add 1 cup of the champagne, reserving 1/4 cup. Stir until **champagne** is completely absorbed.

Begin to add simmering broth 1/2 cup at a time, stirring frequently but waiting until the broth is absorbed before adding more. After 18 to 20 minutes the rice should be tender but still firm. Stir in remaining 1/4 cup of champagne, mushrooms, half and half, **cheese**, and parsley. Serve Immediately. Serves 4.

Champagne Ice

A cool, crisp, and soothing finish. This is a soft pairing of ginger with champagne; if you like ginger, you may want to add more.

3 1/2 cups or one bottle (750 ml) champagne
2 teaspoons freshly grated ginger
5 tablespoons granulated sugar

In a heavy saucepan, combine all ingredients. Cook over moderate heat until the mixture just begins to boil, stirring constantly. Pour into medium-sized stainless steel mixing bowl and cool to room temperature. Place in freezer. After 2 hours, the mixture should have begun to freeze on the sides of the bowl. Scrape frozen ice off the sides toward center of bowl. Repeat this every hour for 3 to 4 hours, until the mixture is like finely crushed ice. Serve in frozen stemmed glasses or bowls. Serves 4.

Bottle Sizes

Split	1/4 bottle
Half	1/2 bottle
Magnum	2 bottles
Jeroboam	4 bottles
Mathusalem	8 bottles
Salmanazar	12 bottles
Balthazar	16 bottles
Nebuchadnezzar	20 bottles

The champagne bottle must be strong to prevent breakage during the second fermentation. The shape facilitates the fall of sediment and the extraction of the cork. The dome-shaped indentation in the bottom of the bottle is called "the punt." It helps to distribute the pressure inside the bottle over a balanced surface area, thereby reducing stress on the bottle. The punt is advantageous for storage because the neck of one bottle fits into the punt of the one behind it.

It is generally thought that champagne is better when it comes from a bigger bottle, perhaps because it has had more room to do what champagne does best—ferment within the bottle.

Stars

"I consider myself more fortunate than most women in that I know several good drinking companions of my own sex. They are for the most part well past seventy, a significant fact in the study of Alcohol in Modern Society. I imagine ... the best of them eighty-two last Christmas has taught me much of both self-control and sensual pleasure from her enjoyment of a glass of dry champagne.

M.F.K. Fisher, *How to Cook a Wolf*

Grapes with Herbed Chèvre and Toasted Almonds

Dry champagne, tangy goat cheese and toasty, buttered nuts create the perfect introduction for a bite of sweet grape.

2 cups red seedless grapes, washed, with stems removed
1/2 cup herbed soft chèvre (goat cheese)
2 tablespoons unsalted butter
2 cloves garlic, finely minced
1 cup toasted almonds, chopped

Roll each **grape** in a small portion of the herbed cheese, so that each grape is coated in a thin layer of cheese. In a medium-sized **sauté** pan, melt the butter. Add the garlic and sauté 1 minute. Add the chopped almonds and sauté another 3 to 4 minutes or until they are a light golden brown. Transfer garlic-almond mixture to a plate and allow to cool. Roll each cheese-coated grape in the **garlic-almond** mixture until coated with a layer of nuts. Serve as an appetizer or tossed gently on top of a green salad. Serves 4 to 6 as an **appetizer**.

Champagne Mint Jelly

Try this light, refreshing jelly on a piece of toast with fresh fruit, or add a bit more mint and serve it with a roasted leg of lamb.

1 1/2 envelopes unflavored gelatin
3/4 cup cold water
1/2 cup granulated sugar
1 bottle (750 ml) dry champagne
1/2 cup fresh mint, chopped

In a medium-sized saucepan, *sprinkle* the gelatin over the water. Let stand 1 minute. Cook over low heat until gelatin is dissolved, stirring constantly. Add the sugar and one half of the champagne, stirring over low heat until the *sugar* is dissolved. Remove the pan from the heat and allow the mixture to cool. Stir in the remaining champagne. Chill for 6 hours or overnight. Before serving, stir in **mint** with a fork, until mixture becomes jelly-like and the mint is evenly distributed. Makes 4 cups.

On special occasions, at the home of a local actor and bon vivant, everyone was drawn into the dining room. As everyone settled themselves, our host arranged a mound of warm sauerkraut on a huge platter in the kitchen. Around this a sort of charcuterie garnie was scattered, with pork chops, smoked meats, and all kinds of sausages. Then in the center of the mound of sauerkraut, a deep indentation was made in which a not-terribly-cold bottle of champagne was nestled. The hood of the bottle was unfastened just seconds before presentation of the platter, and as the warmth of the piquant sauerkraut heated the bubbles, the cork was forced out with a loud and celebratory pop. The champagne spewed all over the pickled cabbage and the meats, blending into a bubbly sauce that married all the flavors.

*T*all, narrow crystal flutes or tulip glasses have for years been the glass of choice for anyone who knows or loves champagne. They conserve the bubbles. Since crystal is slightly rougher than plain glass, more bubbles form in these delicate glasses.

These days it is agreed that the wide bird-bath or saucer-on-a-stem style champagne glass does not enhance the flavor or bubbles of champagne. Nor are these glasses appropriate at big parties, for if someone taps your elbow, out spills the bubbly wine.

Why do we feel such a distinct sense of delight when we walk into a party and are greeted by a silver tray with frosty champagne glasses? The sound alone—the tinkling of the tall flutes—beckons us. We feel taken care of; our hosts have walked the extra mile and dug a little deeper into the pocket to make sure that we'll have a jolly time right from the start. No standing in line at the bar; we start toasting and celebrating practically before we've removed our coats. Blame it on the champagne, but laughter comes a little more fluidly and words—in conversation and toasts—seem better chosen.

Champagne Poached Eggs

This recipe works well with still champagne, for those rare occasions when there is a bit left over. This dish imparts the rich flavor of Eggs Benedict without the heavy sauce.

8 eggs
2 tablespoons unsalted butter
2 cups champagne
8 thin slices smoked salmon
4 thin slices warm, buttered toast
ground black pepper to taste
chopped chives as garnish

In a small saucepan boil 2 cups of water. Place 4 eggs in their shells in the boiling water, count to 30 and then remove them. Repeat. This will help retain their shape in the poaching process. In a small sauté pan, melt the butter. Add the champagne and bring to a simmer. Gently crack each egg over the simmering liquid, letting the egg ease into the pan. Poach each egg for 2 to 2 1/2 minutes; do not crowd the pan. Remove each egg with a slotted spoon. Lay 2 slices of smoked salmon over each slice of toast and place 2 eggs side by side on top. Add freshly ground pepper, a sprinkle of chives, and, if desired, a squeeze of lemon. Serve immediately. Serves 4.

"I let him buy
Only the best.
Madame Clicqu
night i August
along my tongue
brought back

Jeanette Winterson, *The Passion*

me champagne.

I hadn't tasted

t since the hot

The rush of it

d into my throat

her memories."

Cheese & Pepper Cookies

Very rich little bites of cheese, best followed with a cool sip of champagne.

1/2 pound butter
1 1/2 cups of Asiago cheese, grated
2 cups flour
3/4 tablespoon fresh cracked
    pepper (medium to fine grind)
2 teaspoons milk

Preheat oven to 325°F. Cream butter and cheese together; beat well. Sift flour and pepper together. Beat one half dry mixture into butter and cheese; add milk. Mix well. Add remainder of dry mixture and continue to mix well. Roll dough into 1/2 inch round balls. Place balls on cookie sheet. Bake for 25-30 minutes, until golden in color. Makes about 50 cookies.

The swirl of the bubbles hits the optic nerve, the eyelashes, tickles the tip of the nose, and finally explodes in aromatic bouquet on the tongue, exciting the taste buds. Because carbonation makes the flavors of champagne more assertive, intensifying the sweetness and alcohol flavors, grapes are picked when it is cool so the sweetness and alcohol levels will be low. Some vineyards even harvest grapes at night or at first light in the morning so the grapes are cool and consistent in flavor when they are crushed.

A result of carbonic acid in the wine, bubbles are scientifically controlled by the champagne maker so they are busy from the time the fermentation begins until well after they have been sipped. The flute glass keeps the bubbles lively longer than the old-fashioned birdbath glass. In the latter, the bubbles quickly explode because they are widely exposed to air, whereas the shape of a flute glass naturally causes a slower swirling ascent of bubbles. Generally, the better the champagne, the smaller the bubbles—they magnify its subtlety. Small bubbles have a longer life than large ones.

Kir Royale

chilled champagne
a few drops of crème de cassis
a twist of lemon peel

Fill a champagne glass three-quarters full with champagne. Add crème de cassis and stir. Garnish with the lemon peel.

Bellini

1 ripe peach
very cold champagne

Puree the peach in a blender and pour into 2 champagne glasses. Fill glasses with champagne.

Champagne Cocktail

1 cube sugar
a dash of bitters
a twist of lemon peel
chilled champagne

Place the sugar, bitters, and lemon twist in the bottom of a champagne glass. Fill glass with champagne.

Herb Ravioli with Champagne Butter

Delicate wonton wrappers make this a tender pasta. With an uncomplicated champagne, butter sauce, soft cheese, and sage filling, it is lovely in the late evening.

5 tablespoons unsalted butter
3 tablespoons minced shallots
1 1/2 teaspoons minced sage
2 tablespoons chopped parsley
1 cup ricotta cheese
1/2 cup grated Reggiano cheese
1 whole egg
24 wonton wrappers
2 egg whites
3/4 cup champagne
freshly ground pepper to taste
chopped parsley for garnish

In a medium-sized skillet, melt 2 tablespoons of the butter. Add the shallots and sauté until slightly translucent, about 3 minutes. Add the sage and 2 tablespoons of parsley and continue to stir for 1 more minute. Turn off the heat and allow to cool slightly.

Stir in the ricotta, the Reggiano, and the whole egg. Set aside. To make ravioli, take a wonton wrapper, brush its edges with some egg white, and place 1 tablespoon of the cheese mixture in the center. Place another wrapper on top and seal the edges. Repeat for all wrappers.

Bring a large pot of slightly salted water to a boil. Gently place the ravioli in the pot and allow to boil for 3 to 4 minutes or until the squares float to the surface. Remove the ravioli with a slotted spoon and place on warmed plates. In a small saucepan melt the remaining butter and add the champagne. Let the mixture come to a boil and then spoon it over the ravioli. Add a bit of pepper and a sprinkle of parsley and serve. Serves 4 (or 16 large ravioli).

$\mathcal{H}$igh heels sink into the grass, hats flop, men draw handkerchiefs from their pockets to dab their brows. The bride is taking forever. There is not a breeze in the late afternoon summer air. Children are not allowed to romp and muss their clothes until the ceremony is over. The harpsichordist patiently waits for the cue.

Finally that pop of relief echoes out to the garden from the kitchen. Waiters circulate with silver trays that jiggle with glasses filled with champagne. The ice melts; the tension eases. The guests have the unconventional glass before the wedding even begins and then, as if the sky has opened and breathed a sigh of relief, the music begins and the bride ascends.

$\mathcal{I}$t was the mid-sixties in Santiago. Golda Meir was coming to town. The state of Israel was trying to establish the legitimacy of a divided Jerusalem as its capital. It was a time when most countries, including Chile, had embassies in Tel Aviv so as not to offend the Arabs, which in turn, offended the Israelis. The president of Chile had a dilemma. What could he offer to Ms. Meir to make her feel welcome? He asked his close friend and confidant, a prominent Chilean Jew, for suggestions.

"Line a silver tray with beautiful champagne glasses into which pureed raspberries have been poured," offered the confidant. "Then have one of your staff set the tray in front of all the dignitaries. Ask him to open a Jeroboam of Moët et Chandon as soon as you are seated. Fill the glasses. Toast one another. Break the ice. Enliven the air. Then tell her that you would like to move the Embassy of Chile from Tel Aviv to Jerusalem." He guaranteed this would please the formidable head of state, and it did.

Champagne Poached Chocolate Cream Pears

A single poached pear on a dessert plate always makes a whimsical presentation. Add a little chocolate, a herbal hint, and the pair finds a sweet symmetry.

1 bottle (750 ml) champagne
6 sprigs lemon thyme
4 firm, ripe pears
3/4 cup whipping cream
4 tablespoons semi-sweet
   chocolate powder, and a bit
   more for garnish

Pour the champagne into a large saucepan and place covered over low heat. Add the lemon thyme. Peel the pears and slice them in half width-wise. With a melon baller, remove the core from both halves of each pear. Place the bottom halves in the saucepan and cover. After 5 minutes add the top halves and replace lid. Continue to simmer for another 10 minutes.

Remove pears carefully with slotted spoon, then set aside to cool slightly. When cool, trim pear bottoms so pears will stand upright. Reduce poaching liquid for another 10 minutes.

Meanwhile, in a medium-sized mixing bowl, whip the whipping cream until it begins to stiffen. Add 2 tablespoons of the chocolate powder and continue to whip the cream. Add the remainder of the chocolate powder and whip until the cream is stiff. Spoon some chocolate cream into each bottom pear half. Then place a pear top on each chocolate-cream-stuffed bottom. Dust lightly with chocolate powder. Place on dessert plates and spoon a bit of the warm champagne sauce on each plate. Serves 4.

Lemon Olive Crostini

Toast, olives and lemon, fragrantly reminiscent of Summer earth. Cool champagne underscores each subtle flavor.

1 cup green and black olives,
   pitted, chopped
1 tablespoon olive oil
1/2 tablespoon balsamic vinegar
1 tablespoon grated lemon zest
1/2 baguette, sliced thin, or 12 to
   15 small, thin slices of bread
olive oil to drizzle

Preheat oven to 400°F. In a small bowl, combine the olives, 1 tablespoon olive oil, vinegar, and lemon zest. Set mixture aside.

Arrange the bread slices on a baking sheet and drizzle each slice lightly with olive oil. Bake for 10 to 15 minutes or until surfaces are light golden brown. Spoon a small amount of olive mixture over each toast. Serves 3 to 4 as a light appetizer.

Champagne Mignonette

This dipping sauce is a clean complement to the exalted oyster and a glass of champagne.

1 shallot, finely chopped
3 tablespoons champagne
1 1/2 tablespoons rice wine
   vinegar
freshly cracked black peppercorns
   to taste

In a small bowl, combine all ingredients. Allow to stand at room temperature for 10 minutes before refrigerating. Serve chilled. Makes enough to dip at least 24 oysters.

During the night raindrops froze on the dogwood trees outside the creaky leaded windows. We awoke to the faint, persistent tinkling of chimes. The wind had picked up and brushed the frozen branches against one another. Their music sounded like a hundred champagne glasses clinking a toast to the end of the storm.

List of Champagne Recipes

Champagne mint jelly	68
Champagne mignonette	92
Champagne ice	64
Champagne poached salmon	50
Champagne grilled leeks	55
Champagne risotto with wild mushrooms	59
Herb ravioli with champagne butter	85
Champagne poached eggs	75
Champagne melon with smoked trout	45
Champagne poached chocolate cream pears	94

Recipes to accompany champagne

Grilled nectarines with prosciutto	24
Cheese & pepper cookies	79
Grapes with herbed chèvre and toasted almonds	67
Lemon olive crostini	92

Champagne drinks

Kir royale	82
Bellini	82
Champagne cocktail	82